30 DAYS TO UNSHAKABLE PEACE

A Daily Journey to Calm and Clarity

by
Reverend Virginia S. Walker

Published by Mid Atlanta Book Publishing
Atlanta, Georgia

Copyright © 2025 by
Reverend Virginia S. Walker
All rights reserved.

No part of this publication may be reproduced, distributed, or transmitted in any form or by any means, including photocopying, recording, or other electronic or mechanical methods, without the prior written permission of the publisher, except in the case of brief quotations used in critical reviews and certain other noncommercial uses permitted by copyright law.

30 Days to Unshakable Peace
ISBN: 979-8-9936892-0-3

Published by Mid Atlanta Book Publishing
Atlanta, Georgia

Scripture quotations are from the New Revised Standard Version Bible, copyright © 1989 National Council of the Churches of Christ in the United States of America. Used by permission. All rights reserved.

INTRODUCTION

In a world filled with noise, pressure, and uncertainty, peace can sometimes feel just out of reach. Yet, God's Word reminds us that peace is not something we must chase. It is a promise we can live in every day.

This 30 day devotional was created to help you draw closer to the heart of God, one quiet moment at a time. Each day offers Scripture, reflection, prayer, and a simple "peace practice" to help you live out God's promises in real, practical ways. Whether you're beginning your day with Him or winding down before rest, these readings are designed to renew your mind and calm your spirit.

Unshakable peace doesn't mean life will always be easy. It means that, through faith, you can remain steady when everything around you feels uncertain. Over the next thirty days, you'll be invited to surrender your worries, trust God's timing, and rest in His presence.

As you move through each page, take your time. Breathe deeply. Let the words sink in. Reflect, write, and listen for God's whisper in your heart.

May this devotional be a gentle reminder that peace is already yours through Christ. A peace the world cannot give and cannot take away.

Reverend Virginia S. Walker

To everyone who chooses faith over fear, and peace over pressure.

———————————————

Day 1

Peace Begins with Surrender

'He will keep in perfect peace those whose minds are steadfast, because they trust in Him.'

Scripture: Isaiah 26:3

Reflection

Peace doesn't start when life gets easier. It starts when you stop fighting for control. God promises peace to those whose hearts are anchored in Him. Today, release the need to fix everything on your own. Trust that what you surrender, He will sustain.

Prayer

Lord, I surrender the battles I've been carrying. Teach me to trust You with every outcome. Help me to stay steadfast in faith, not in fear. Amen.

Peace Practice

Write down three worries and say out loud:
'God, I give this to You.'

Day 2

Guarding Your Heart and Mind

'And the peace of God, which transcends all understanding, will guard your hearts and your minds in Christ Jesus.'

Scripture: Philippians 4:7

Reflection

God's peace is like a shield. It doesn't always remove the storm, but it guards you through it. When chaos tries to overwhelm your thoughts, pause and invite His presence in. You don't need all the answers. All you need is His calm assurance.

Prayer

Father, when my mind races, quiet my spirit. Wrap me in Your peace that surpasses understanding. Amen.

Peace Practice

Breathe deeply for 60 seconds. With each breath, whisper 'Jesus.' Let your body rest in His stillness. Then write down 3 things you are grateful for.

_____
_____
_____
_____
_____
_____
_____
_____
_____
_____
_____
_____

Day 3

Letting Go of 'What Ifs'

'Therefore do not worry about tomorrow, for tomorrow will worry about itself. Each day has enough trouble of its own.'

Scripture: Matthew 6:34

Reflection

Anxious thoughts often live in the future, in the land of 'what if.' But peace lives in the now. God gives strength for today. When you catch yourself drifting toward tomorrow's worries, return to this moment. You are safe, loved, and provided for right here.

Prayer

God, help me to release tomorrow into Your hands. Remind me that Your grace meets me daily, not all at once. Amen.

Peace Practice

Every time you say 'what if' today, follow it with 'even if. Write down ways you are reminded that God is still in control.'

_____
_____
_____
_____
_____
_____
_____
_____
_____
_____
_____
_____
_____
_____
_____

Day 4

When Worry Knocks

'Come to me, all you who are weary and burdened, and I will give you rest.'

Scripture: Matthew 11:28

Reflection

Worry will always knock, but you decide whether it stays. Jesus invites you to trade heavy thoughts for His rest. When anxiety rises, picture yourself handing each concern to Him like stones dropped from your hands. The lighter your grip, the easier His peace can fill the space.

Prayer

Lord, when my thoughts grow heavy, remind me to bring them straight to You. Exchange my worry for Your rest. Amen.

Peace Practice

Every time you catch yourself worrying, pause and whisper, 'I give this to You, Jesus.'

Day 5

The Still Voice

'And after the fire came a gentle whisper.'

Scripture: 1 Kings 19:12

Reflection

God's peace rarely shouts. It whispers. The world's noise can drown out His calm direction unless you choose silence. Take time today to turn off distractions and listen. His voice is gentle but steady, and it always leads you back to peace.

Prayer

Father, teach me to quiet the noise around me so I can hear Your gentle whisper. Amen.

Peace Practice

Spend five minutes in total silence today. No phone, no music. Just breathe and listen then write down what is revealed to you.

_____
_____
_____
_____
_____
_____
_____
_____
_____
_____
_____
_____

Day 6

Peace in the Waiting

'Wait for the Lord; be strong and take heart and wait for the Lord.'

Scripture: Psalm 27:14

Reflection

Waiting can feel like standing still, but in God's timing, waiting builds strength. Peace comes not from what you see but from who you trust. When answers delay, remember, God never wastes your wait.

Prayer

Lord, help me rest in Your perfect timing. While I wait, grow my faith stronger than my frustration. Amen.

Peace Practice

Write one thing you're waiting for and declare aloud, 'God is working while I wait.'

_____
_____
_____
_____
_____
_____
_____
_____
_____
_____
_____
_____
_____
_____

Day 7

Choosing Peace Over People Pleasing

'Am I now trying to win the approval of human beings, or of God?'

Scripture: Galatians 1:10

Reflection

When you chase everyone's approval, peace slips through your fingers. True calm comes from knowing you already have God's approval. You don't have to perform for His love. He gives it freely.

Prayer

God, free me from the pressure to please everyone. Let Your approval be enough for me. Amen.

Peace Practice

Say NO once today where you normally would've said YES. Notice the peace that follows.

Day 8

The Anchor in the Storm

'We have this hope as an anchor for the soul, firm and secure.'

Scripture: Hebrews 6:19

Reflection

Storms test what anchors you. When emotions toss you around, hope in Christ keeps you steady. The winds may howl, but your soul can stay still when anchored in His promise.

Prayer

Jesus, be my anchor when life feels uncertain. Keep me grounded in Your Word and not in my fears. Amen.

Peace Practice

Write down three verses that anchor you.
Keep them visible all week.

_____
_____
_____
_____
_____
_____
_____
_____
_____
_____
_____
_____
_____
_____

Day 9

Release the Outcome

'In their hearts humans plan their course, but the Lord establishes their steps.'

Scripture: Proverbs 16:9

Reflection

Peace fades when we try to script every detail. God's direction is better than our design. Today, let go of needing to know how everything ends. Just trust the One who already does.

Prayer

Lord, help me release control and rest in Your plan. Align my steps with Your will. Amen.

Peace Practice

Pray this simple line throughout your day:
'God, I trust Your outcome more than my own.'

Day 10

Resting in His Goodness

'Surely Your goodness and love will follow me all the days of my life.'

Scripture: Psalm 23:6

Reflection

God's goodness doesn't come and go with your feelings. It follows you daily. Even when life feels heavy, His mercy trails close behind. When you stop chasing peace and start resting in His goodness, you'll realize it's been beside you all along.

Prayer

Father, thank You that Your goodness never leaves me. Help me to rest, knowing You're always near. Amen.

Peace Practice

List three ways you've seen God's goodness this week, no matter how small.

_____
_____
_____
_____
_____
_____
_____
_____
_____
_____
_____
_____
_____

Day 11

Peace in the Unknown

'Be still and know that I am God.'

Scripture: Psalm 46:10

Reflection

Uncertainty can make us restless, but peace is found in stillness. God doesn't ask you to have all the answers—only to trust that He does. When the future feels unclear, remember that He sees the road ahead and walks with you through every step.

Prayer

Lord, teach me to rest when I cannot see the outcome. Let my faith grow stronger than my fear. Amen.

Peace Practice

Spend five minutes today in complete stillness. Breathe deeply and repeat the words, 'Be still, and know.'

Day 12

Let Peace Rule

'Let the peace of Christ rule in your hearts.'

Scripture: Colossians 3:15

Reflection

Peace is not just a feeling, it's a decision. Each day, you choose whether fear or faith will lead you. When you let peace rule, you invite God to take the throne of your emotions, guiding your reactions with grace.

Prayer

Father, let Your peace be my guide today. Help me respond to others with calm and compassion. Amen.

Peace Practice

Before making a decision, pause and ask, 'Will this bring me peace or take it away?'

Day 13

The Gift of Rest

'My presence will go with you, and I will give you rest.'

Scripture: Exodus 33:14

Reflection

True rest isn't found in a weekend away. It's found in the presence of God. When your soul feels tired, step into His presence through prayer, worship, or quiet reflection. He promises rest not just for your body, but for your spirit.

Prayer

Lord, thank You for being my resting place. Quiet my heart and renew my strength in You. Amen.

Peace Practice

Take ten minutes today to do something that calms your spirit. Sit outside, listen to soft music, or journal a prayer.

_____
_____
_____
_____
_____
_____
_____
_____
_____
_____
_____
_____
_____
_____

Day 14

Holding On to Hope

'May the God of hope fill you with all joy and peace as you trust in Him.'

Scripture: Romans 15:13

Reflection

Hope and peace walk hand in hand. When you anchor your hope in God's promises, your heart becomes steady. Even in disappointment, He is still working for your good.

Prayer

God of hope, fill me with peace that surpasses my circumstances. Help me to trust You completely. Amen.

Peace Practice

Write down one area of your life where you need renewed hope. Pray over it daily this week.

_____
_____
_____
_____
_____
_____
_____
_____
_____
_____
_____

Day 15

The Power of Gratitude

'Give thanks in all circumstances.'

Scripture: 1 Thessalonians: 5:18

Reflection

Gratitude is the gateway to peace. It shifts your focus from what's missing to what's present. Every blessing—big or small—is a reminder that God is with you and working on your behalf.

Prayer

Father, thank You for the gifts I often overlook. Open my eyes to see Your goodness around me. Amen.

Peace Practice

List five things you're thankful for today, no matter how simple.

_____
_____
_____
_____
_____
_____
_____
_____
_____
_____
_____
_____
_____
_____

Day 16

Faith Over Fear

'Do not fear, for I am with you; do not be dismayed, for I am your God.'

Scripture: Isaiah 41:10

Reflection

Fear whispers 'you can't,' but faith declares 'God can.' Peace comes when you believe that His presence is greater than your problems. Whatever you face, you're never facing it alone.

Prayer

Lord, replace my fear with faith. Remind me that You are always with me. Amen.

Peace Practice

Each time fear rises today, say aloud, 'God is with me. Therefore I have peace.'

Day 17

Guard Your Thoughts

'Take captive every thought to make it obedient to Christ.'

Scripture: 2 Corinthians 10:5

Reflection

Peace begins in the mind. When you guard your thoughts, you guard your heart. Not every thought deserves your attention. Only the ones rooted in truth and love.

Prayer

God, help me take every anxious thought captive. Fill my mind with what is pure, true, and peaceful. Amen.

Peace Practice

Write down one recurring negative thought, and next to it, write a verse that speaks truth over it.

_____
_____
_____
_____
_____
_____
_____
_____
_____
_____
_____
_____
_____
_____
_____
_____

Day 18

The Strength in Surrender

'Be still before the Lord and wait patiently for Him.'

Scripture: Psalm 37:7

Reflection

Surrender isn't weakness; it's strength in disguise. Letting go of control opens the door for God's peace to flow freely. When you release your grip, He begins to move.

Prayer

Lord, teach me to surrender what I cannot change. I choose to trust Your timing and Your way. Amen.

Peace Practice

Visualize handing your biggest worry to God. Take a deep breath and feel the weight lift.

Day 19

God's Presence in the Everyday

'The Lord your God will be with you wherever you go.'

Scripture: Joshua 1:9

Reflection

Peace isn't only for quiet moments. It's for every moment. God walks with you in the grocery store, in traffic, at work, and at home. When you become aware of His presence, ordinary days become sacred.

Prayer

Thank You, Lord, that You are always with me. Help me sense Your presence in every part of my day. Amen.

Peace Practice

Pause three times today and say, 'God is here.'
Let that awareness bring calm to your spirit.

Day 20

Overflowing Peace

'Peace I leave with you; my peace I give you.'

Scripture: John 14:27

Reflection

Jesus didn't promise a life without problems, but He promised His peace. The peace He gives is complete. It can't be taken by circumstance or stolen by fear. Receive it fully today and let it overflow into how you treat others.

Prayer

Jesus, thank You for the gift of Your peace. Help me carry it wherever I go. Amen.

Peace Practice

Show kindness to someone today through a smile, a prayer, or a simple act of service. Let peace flow through you.

Day 21

Standing Firm in Faith

'Be on your guard; stand firm in the faith; be courageous; be strong.'

Scripture: 1 Corinthians 16:13

Reflection

Peace doesn't mean passivity. It means standing calmly in confidence when life shakes. Faith is your foundation, and when it's rooted in God's Word, you can stand firm even when storms rise around you.

Prayer

Lord, give me strength to stand firm when life feels uncertain. Let my peace rest on Your promises, not my feelings. Amen.

Peace Practice

When something challenges you today, pause and silently repeat: 'I will stand firm in faith.'

Day 22

The Promise of Perfect Timing

'He has made everything beautiful in its time.'

Ecclesiastes 3:11

Reflection

Impatience often steals peace. God's timing rarely matches our schedule, but His timing is always perfect. When you release the urge to rush, you open space for His peace to flow.

Prayer

Father, teach me to trust Your timing. Help me wait with faith instead of worry. Amen.

Peace Practice

Write down one area where you're waiting on God. Next to it, write: 'He is making it beautiful in His time.'

_____
_____
_____
_____
_____
_____
_____
_____
_____
_____
_____
_____

Day 23

Rest for a Weary Heart

'Take my yoke upon you and learn from me, for I am gentle and humble in heart, and you will find rest for your souls.'

Scripture: Matthew 11:29

Reflection

Jesus offers rest, not just relief. His peace goes deeper than sleep. It quiets the noise in your heart. When you lean on Him, He carries what you were never meant to bear alone.

Prayer

Gentle Savior, thank You for offering rest to my soul. Teach me to lean on You daily. Amen.

Peace Practice

Spend five minutes today sitting quietly with your hand over your heart. Breathe deeply and whisper, 'Lord, give me rest.'

Day 24

Living Above the Noise

'In quietness and trust is your strength.'

Scripture: Isaiah 30:15

Reflection

The world glorifies busyness, but peace is found in quiet. God's strength is revealed not in your striving but in your stillness. When you slow down, you make room to hear His voice.

Prayer

Lord, help me quiet the noise of the world. Let my strength be found in trusting You. Amen.

Peace Practice

Turn off all media for one hour today. Use that time to rest or pray in silence.

Day 25
A Calm Spirit

'A heart at peace gives life to the body.'

Scripture: Proverbs 14:30

Reflection

Stress affects the spirit and the body. When your heart is at peace, your whole being benefits. Guard your heart. It's a gift from God that renews both your mind and body.

Prayer

God, calm my heart and renew my strength. Let Your peace bring life to my body and joy to my spirit. Amen.

Peace Practice

Take a slow walk outside and thank God for every breath, step, and heartbeat.

Day 26
Letting God Defend You

'The Lord will fight for you; you need only to be still.'

Scripture: Exodus 14:14

Reflection

You don't have to fight every battle. Some victories are won through stillness, not fighting. Peace comes when you trust that God defends you better than you can defend yourself.

Prayer

Lord, I release the need to prove or protect myself. Fight for me as only You can. Amen.

Peace Practice

When conflict or misunderstanding arises, choose silence and prayer instead of reaction.

Day 27

Strength in Gentleness

'Let your gentleness be evident to all. The Lord is near.'

Scripture: Philippians 4:5

Reflection

Gentleness is not weakness. It's strength under control. Peaceful people carry power because they don't let emotions dictate their actions. When you respond gently, you reflect God's heart.

Prayer

Father, teach me to respond with gentleness even when I feel misunderstood. Let my peace point others to You. Amen.

Peace Practice

Speak softly today. Even when frustrated, lower your tone and breathe before you respond.

Day 28

Unmovable Peace

'Truly He is my rock and my salvation; He is my fortress, I will not be shaken.'

Scripture: Psalm 62:6

Reflection

True peace doesn't depend on calm circumstances. It's rooted in an unshakable God. When the ground beneath you feels unstable, remember who your fortress is.

Prayer

Lord, You are my rock. Keep me steady when life feels uncertain. Amen.

Peace Practice

Write this verse somewhere you'll see it often:
'I will not be shaken.'

Day 29
Joy in the Morning

'Weeping may stay for the night, but rejoicing comes in the morning.'

Scripture: Psalm 30:5

Reflection

Every dark night eventually gives way to morning light. God's peace reminds you that no pain lasts forever. Hope rises with the dawn, bringing strength for a new day.

Prayer

God, thank You that joy comes after sorrow. Help me hold on to hope through the night. Amen.

Peace Practice

Wake up early tomorrow and watch the sunrise. Let it remind you that new beginnings always come.

Day 30

The Peace That Remains

'In this world you will have trouble. But take heart! I have overcome the world.'

Scripture: John 16:33

Reflection

Peace doesn't disappear when life gets hard. It remains because Jesus remains. He overcame every fear, sorrow, and challenge so that you could live with peace that endures through it all.

Prayer

Jesus, thank You for overcoming the world. Help me to rest in Your victory and walk in unshakable peace. Amen.

Peace Practice

End your day by thanking God for three ways He has carried you this month.

_____
_____
_____
_____
_____
_____
_____
_____
_____
_____
_____
_____
_____

Day 31

Reflection & Gratitude

Reflection

Take time today to look back over the past 30 days. Reflect on how God has met you in moments of worry, stillness, and faith. Peace is not a destination but a daily walk with Him. As you move forward, carry these truths in your heart and let His calm continue to guide you.

Prayer

Lord, thank You for teaching me to find peace in Your presence. Let this peace remain within me and flow through me to others. Amen.

Notes

Notes

About The Author

Reverend Virginia S. Walker's journey of faith and service is a testament to her unwavering dedication to God and her community. A lifelong learner and spiritual leader, she has devoted her career to ministry, education, and compassionate care.

Reverend Walker graduated from Denmark Olar High School in 1976 and earned a diploma in Early Childhood Development from Denmark Technical College in 1991. She later achieved an Associate's degree in Human Services (2003) and a Bachelor's degree in Organizational Management from Claflin University (2007). Her theological education includes a Bachelor's degree in Theology (2013) and a Master's degree from Carolina Theological Bible Institute (2018).

Reverend Walker has faithfully served in various ministry roles, including Interim Pastor at Rome Baptist Church, where she provided spiritual leadership and care. She is currently the Associate Pastor at Rome Baptist Church in Denmark, South Carolina, where she continues to guide and inspire the congregation.

Beyond the pulpit, Reverend Walker serves as an on-call Chaplain at the Medical University of South Carolina, offering prayer and comfort to patients and families in need. In 2023, she became a Certified Life Coach. Her educational accomplishments, ordination, and extensive experience as a minister and chaplain highlight her deep commitment to serving others. Her faith, compassion, and continuous pursuit of growth embody her mission to uplift, encourage, and share the peace of Christ with all.

Reverend Walker resides in South Carolina with her husband of 45 years. They are the loving parents and grandparents to six children and twelve grandchildren.

www.ingramcontent.com/pod-product-compliance
Lightning Source LLC
Chambersburg PA
CBHW042303150426
43196CB00005B/64